This book is dedicated to Sarah -
Thank you for everything you have created;
In addition to blessing me with three beautiful and intelligent
children, you have also instilled significant faith in me
and you have remained my deepest inspiration.
All of which has given me purpose,
as well as dreams to achieve.
You created all of it.
I am forever
grateful.

Published by:
Powder River Publishing LLC
1014 Black Mountain Road
Thermopolis, Wyoming 82443

Copyright © 2024
ISBN: 978-1-956881-48-6
Printed in the United States of America

Powder River Publishing

www.powderriverpublishing.com

Table of contents

Expressions

I don't rap or sing, play the keys or strings;
Although my mind is instrumental.
Similar release; self-therapy sessions.
Advantageous over detrimental.
I relish writing in rhythmic fashion,
My expressions of creative passion.
Where in any place or mood, time of day or night,
It can be done, or inspiration.
I write down a word and line-up a phrase,
Ironically, to follow another.
Seemingly meant to rhyme.
Rewrote countless times.
To become titled, owned, and uttered.

Unrivaled Wilderness

To the marvelous mountain that stands before me,
And before mankind was ever a hope,
I was born beneath you in '87,
Under the eye of your eastern slope.
My visits may be sparsely spread but I see you all the damn time.
Even daydreams are deeply embedded within the shade of your
dense pines.
Mesmerized by your constant beauty,
Each curve enhanced by the changing light.
From your snow capped peaks to canyon walls,
Everything naturally placed just right.
Your creeks and streams run through my mind, inundating stress
and pain.
Precipices that you possess are perfect for tossing angst away.
You've given me shelter from your own damn storms,
Even whilst they are still raging.
Memories captured in your neck of the woods,
Are steel-trapped, and still amaze me.
You have fed my hunger.
You have quenched my thirst.
You've tried to kill me, yet kept me alive.
When it comes to the promised land, I think of you first.
Without you, I'm rapture deprived.
Oh, Bighorn Mountains of wondrous Wyoming,
And that serrated silhouette you bear,
Not only are you unrivaled wilderness,
But a faultless disguise for Heaven's stairs.

Boots to Brim

From boots to brim, it comes from within; How young cowboys possess old souls.
Perhaps weathered leather and worn straw hats carry more than you've been told.
It's our way of life not just our look, though clearly, some not aught know,
The desire and need for the things we wear, work with, drive, and sow.
It's farming and ranching, working and playing, hunting and fishing outside.
Actual sunlight. Actual clouds.
Actual statewide-loving pride.
In blistering-cold horizontal-snow to sweltering high-desert heat,
We take advantage of fusing with water, or the land beneath our feet.
Time in town simply keeps us down. The mountains pick us up;
Barely lifting a finger to raise our spirits, to fish, hunt, play and love.

Trapped in the Past

His long-lost soul found land to furrow;
At last, he is settled down.
He came up from Carolina, blew into Tennessee,
Leaving the hell in that small town.
Spent the winter in The Land of Blue Smoke,
Then sprung out West in early Spring.
Homesteadily dreaming to bed beneath,
Rugged mountains in Wyoming.
The Cowboy State seemed equally as great,
As to any place on all God's earth.
Generously placed to face views of Heaven,
All so evenly dispersed.
And as luck would have it, this man built his cabin,
Not too far from an old fur-trapper.
To pick new peaks, or his new-friend's quaint-mind?
He obviously chose the latter.
Yet honored with both, as they'd trek trails,
Together amid the mountain;
He and a trapper, trapped by time.
Snared in a pastime that bound them.

Buffalo Rose

Sailing amidst the lowly badlands,
Across high prairie plains.
Land of lumps, like piled laundry,
Under cover of cold-snapped sage.
Ebb and flow through drifted snow,
Cut by weathered-wheels of a prairie schooner.
Looking forward to springtime's arrival;
Wishing it could bound-in sooner.
Anchored down between wildlife and natives.
Each accustomed to running the land.
And thrice the struggle to eat dwindled rations,
If the frost bites both his hands.
Two kids and a wife. Both folks from both sides.
Eight hungry mouths to feed.
With a busted flintlock, he wields a primal bow,
And a Bowie knife from a pronghorn sheath.
Spot and stalk; envisioning the drop,
Of the most fascinating ungulate known.
Daring to down the body of the beast...
On the frontier where the buffalo rose.

Reins of Mane

Rustlers wrangled a handful of horses;
Making off with the rancher's pride.
But he heard the bustle and grabbed his rifle;
Commencing his own midnight ride.
A galvanized man in hot pursuit,
Across cold moonlit plains.
Hell bent on bareback. No time for leather.
White-knuckling reins of mane.
If he catches one then he could catch all,
The other outlaws' worthless names.
He hears the thunder under their hooves.
Not a whole lot left to gain.
Clouds crash in, and soaked the sky;
Dry-gulched the prairie with pounding rain.
He's hot on their tail, and leveling steel,
As his clinched-legs light-up with pain.
With three in his sight, lightning strikes.
One of the rustlers mired in mud.
Struck in a lung; ending his run;
Coughing up names in blood.

Tears Upon Tin Roofs

To: Earth Below. From: Angel Eyes.
Tears drop to end the drought.
Pouring down atop peaks and valleys,
Halting the last straw of doubt.
Filling fields and flowing ditches.
Spouting out from house and barn.
Tears plinking upon tin roofs;
The instrumental anthem on the farm.
To hear and feel them once again,
Rejuvenates a weathered soul.
For their fall all else shall rise,
To the occasion for the crops to grow.

Benevolent Mountains

I wake each day and see the same face,
Well prior to my aging-own.
Complexion of dirt, trees, and prairie grass,
Sagebrush, snowpack, and stone.
Beautiful creations that may seem cruel.
Thirteen-thousand feet and counting.
With pane between us, out my bedroom window,
Stand benevolent mountains.
Peaceful and kind, yet fierce and wild.
Having withstood the test of time.
Strewn out peaks and countless valleys.
Flora gives life, for that, fauna survives.
Reaching so high that the clouds seem low;
Brushing Blacktooth damn near daily.
Many crags, creeks, and deep canyon steeps,
Are all hidden in sight before me.
Most of the land is untouched by hand,
Or the foot of man, it's so remote.
Sunshine, fog, shadows, and frost,
Wind, rain, sleet, hail, and snow,
Reaching places; natural nooks and crannies,
Where wildlife thrive, not humans.
Which should remind us to leave no trace,
Of undesired mankind attributions.

Cow Shit For Credence

Sidewinding and slithering, moseying on,
Meandering through the badlands.
I've been sitting here with a birds-eye-view,
Watching from sandstone grandstands.
The same Bighorn River that was carried through,
A quaint canyon by the Wind.
Now outside Greybull, next to me,
Beneath its water-shedding kin.
The Bighorn Mountains standing tall.
Clouds catching all the peaks.
Flashing snowcaps, each to the other;
Brilliant bouncing sunlight beams.
Partly overcast parting bright blue sky.
Good for shadow racing across the plains.
Mine's moving more at pace with the Sun;
A slow change in remaining the same.
Slight breeze makes way across sage seas,
Hence subtle waves of prairie grass.
Jackrabbits, lizards, field mice and snakes,
Look to keep intact, the eagle's fast.
Where speed goats, coyotes, and deer duly roam,
Yip-howl and run wild for free,
Cow shit for credence, I am, indeed,
Sitting in Cowboy Country.

Hope Floats

Tried and true. Time-tested fortitude.
Living life below a brim.
Black and blue. Scraped and bruised.
Yet, he would do it all again.
The exact same way he'd done before,
For each scar and every stitch.
He's pitched the hay every single day;
Giddyin' up without a hitch.
For a lifetime now, he's shown how,
A cowboy gets shit done.
Home on the range ain't a game,
Albeit he beats the rising sun.
Each morning his boots hit the floor,
Long before the light.
Heads out the door with nothing more,
Than a .44 and his pocket knife.
Carrying pain with poise. Pride with passion.
Yet, stress with added strain.
Not from a deal he made with the devil.
It's from a deal that he made with rain.
There've been years of doubt.
Years of drought.
Some years were clearly both.
But he's kept his hands firmly on this land,
By keeping hope afloat.

Wyomingite

The mountains and prairies feathered across the frontier are masterpieces on God's easel.
He paints them full, with his brilliant touch, of guns, His grace, and good people.
Friendly faces, one wouldn't want to face, if one disrespected the name.
But lends a hand in demand of hope, even to bury hatchets in the clay.
A heavenly haven most of the year; His home-away-from-home.
Yet, when winter hits we're on our own, so we create angels in the snow.
His favorite creatures and landscape features are strewn throughout this land.
From Yellowstone to Devils Tower; the glory to His keen hand.
We love it here for the reasons most don't; it's cold; it's windy; it's baron.
That culls out the weak, and hardens our edges.
Cuts right through any pretending.
It's hard-work by the people, and our small towns that we're proud of.
We all thank God when the wild calls, so we answer, Hallelujah.
Sitting on our tables are bottles and Bibles. Loaded under them, a .357.
Guns around here are a part of the family; generational; past and present.
Weatherby, Ruger, and Colt are the names. Bolt, lever-action, and singles; the game.
Our pride is as high as the peaks in our sky, and our faith is all the same.

Cowboy Code

From sunup to sundown, he leaves it all out there,
Except for the dirt he tracks back home.
He busts his ass to build a life worth living.
That's all he has ever known.
Keeping food on the table, clothes on his kids,
Fuel in the car, and warmth in the crib.
He checks on the rest of his family and friends.
At the tailend of his list is him.
If he says he will do it, he has gone and done it.
His word is lock-and-key.
He doesn't cheat, won't steal or lie.
He simply lives by a code he bleeds.
Principles known as The Cowboy Code;
Ethics of the West; or Wyoming Way.
He rides for the brand.
Talks less and says more.
Won't let the line get carried away.
He's tough, yet fair. Owns courage and pride.
He knows some things are not for sale.
Does the things that have to be done,
Even if it only brings him hell.
He possesses grit with grace, guns, and guts;
The fortitude to defend thy own.
Exercises selflessness and discipline;
Maintained beyond the age of old.
Shows gratitude and appreciation,
Every time they can be shown.
Not just to others, but to his abled body,
And to the privilege of bringing dirt home.

The Banks

Like each bank forged by an undying river;
Flanking the mountain's pride.
Amidst vivacious emerald meadows.
Lined by pines beneath brilliant skies.
Taking turns, carving out earth.
A varying span between them at times.
Though you can't get one without the other.
Nature's pen has drawn the line.
If not the banks, then I'm the water,
She's the slope that carries me.
If not the banks, then I'm a bluebird,
Taking shelter, 'cause she's the trees,
If not the banks, I'm a forget-me-not seed,
Floating on her, the springtime breeze.
Seems all I need, to the utmost degree,
Is for her to share a life with me.

Forever Endeavour

Waking up grateful every day,
Within a Square State of mind.
Forever West in Wyoming,
For what I can hope is that much time.
My forever endeavor is simple;
Be proud of what I've done.
Keep looking up to reach new heights.
Take care of the ones I love.
This forever endeavor will duly take time.
In turn I've embraced the climb.
Not Too fast.
Not too slow.
But merely a persistent rise and shine.

Powder River Wild

Cold water flowing steady and strong.
'Tis that time of year again.
Snowmelt drops from the mountain top.
Summertime's around the bend.
Life on the rise to warmer skies;
A Spring revival of Powder River.
Rain is falling, but the wild's still calling,
For sweat and pain through late-forever.
A frontier-mile between the banks.
Yet, superficial as a shallow grave.
A country-smile that'll swallow you up,
And her curves go on for days.
The coyotes sing to her every night,
Upon moonlit ridges and rock piles.
Out on the range it's always open,
And stays Powder River wild.
Where big city lights can't hold a candle,
To backwoods bonfire nights.
The river passes quicker than time,
And the prairie moon is hanging tight.
With stars to gaze, looking up and away,
From dancing hypnotic flames.
Sense the presence of old outlaws,
As Wyoming wind whispers their names.
But once the cold draws near and Fall shifts gears,
The snow ain't very far.
Mother Nature starts looking to pin you down,
No matter who you think you are.
You'd better be tough, because it will be rough,
Going rounds against Old Man Winter.
Prepare for the worst.
Respect the wild.
Fear God and Powder River.

Wild Drifter

He was born in Oklahoma.
Made his way to Tennessee.
With his family when he was nine,
Back in 1983.
A decade later, after tragedy,
He watched them lay his mama down.
So it's been years since he's been here,
As he no longer comes around.
The legend goes, he headed West one night,
With his heart barely intact.
With nothing but the clothes he was wearing,
And a handmade-pack upon his back.
The mountains, now, are where he lives,
I hope he outlasts another winter.
We hear his name from time to time,
But he is known as The Wild Drifter.
That grave day seemed to pave the way,
In which he started walking.
He just hit the road,
Couldn't care less it snowed.
No one tried to stop him.
His heart was set on the Rocky Mountains,
Ever since he was a boy.
Way back when his burnt out father,
Played with whiskey like a toy.
And he never really knew who his sister was,
Too many years were in between.
She ran off, once she quit school.
Long-gone somewhere overseas.
The only friends he had ever had,
Were two brothers that moved away.
He is a lone wolf, through and through;
Living in a Wyoming mountain range.

Buffalo

Mountains playing peak-a-boo, from over yonder looking down.
Overseeing a simple and quiet rustic little town.
Western ways from long gone days; Cowboy to the core.
Buried in rich history; proven by an infamous cattle war.
Breathtaking views, and open air, alike your eyes as beauty's seen.
Snow melts down; eastward bound. Clear Creek water flows between.
Kind and fair, the locals there. Living life accordingly.
Shooting you straight in this Square State, known as Equality.
Surrounding allure astounds the mind, as it takes one by the hand.
Leads on-out, on-up, or over; elevating to higher land.
Bighorn Mountains protrude blue skies, reaching for any clouds.
Trees for days in landscaped ways, that must make God so proud.
Wilderness living; a wild life. Welcome to nature's home.
After-all, the forest belongs to the elk and all that roam.
Lakes, rivers, creeks and streams; water all around.
Fowl play. A hunter's dream. And the fishing is profound.
So grab a pole. Drift a fly. Catch a sun tan and a whopper.
Clean it up; Fish to fry. Or release back to the water.
Take a hike, or ride a bike. Spin a bottle for direction.
Up or down. In or out. Either way, Heaven's detected.
Mother Nature did her best, when she raised that little town.
No wonder why we choose to roam where Buffalo settled down.

Sunset Ride

Sitting tall, he had seen it all,
Through his calico eyes beneath a brim.
High in the saddle for eighty-six years,
Among Mother Nature, his wife, and kids.
A man as rugged as the Bighorn Mountains,
With heart as vast as open range.
Raised livestock to make a living,
Through Wyoming winters, aches, and pains.
Now his time has come. He's grabbed his gloves.
He's saddled up in that big blue sky.
Grabbing the reins and tipping his hat.
Taking off on his sunset ride.

Live-on-Location

Way up down a long back road,
On a hill beneath the stars.
The girls are dancing like these flames of fire,
While us boys are falling hard.
We're laying low while getting high,
But things won't get too crazy.
Another cord of wood for another night,
Mixed with Wyoming Whiskey.
The fire helps light the moonlit sky.
Whiskey welcomes celebration.
Good friends around. Crackling fire sounds.
Here; Live-on-location.
To the ones out here at the spot tonight,
Thanks for coming to the show.
Front row seats to bonfire heat,
And the drinks are always cold.
Clouds may creep in from the West,
But if by chance it does start storming,
We might move inside, but like the rain,
The whiskey keeps on pouring.

Wildflower

Out in the middle of an open heart, where romance loves to run,
Lies a being with such vibrant beauty, she rivals the winter sun.
Her touch is soft, like a velvet rose petal, yet as strong as hurricane wind.
So down-to-earth from deep within. You'd think loving her's a sin.
This wildflower may seem fragile but she's a fire on the prairie.
Sight for sore eyes. She disengages my mind; a tantalizing trance upon me.
This wildflower, in a field of desire, has made all my dreams come true.
The magic she holds. Her love, so bold. Casting her light like a perigee moon.
Out of any flower strewn up a mountain, any mountain, she tops them all.
My wildflower holds all the power. All year-long; winter through fall.
Her brilliance glows for miles around but her green eyes are my heart's beacon.
Like an oasis out in the desert, she draws in what I am needing.
Try to tame her allure; impossible. You've a better chance at Yellowstone.
To match her spirit, only God comes near it. And He picked me to watch her grow.
When tempted by the wind her hips start swaying to Mother Nature's careless charm.
Reaching for the stars. Encased by the wild. Holding up her loving arms.

Cloud Peak

Feeling low like an August creek. I headed up beyond the pines.
Looked to raise my spirits as I climbed. Free my mind amongst blue skies.
Prairie grass dancing, like an emerald sea, flooding a sun-strewn meadow.
So I'm out here with the summer breeze, setting sail to The Silverado.
My plan's to get higher than old Cloud Peak, atop the Bighorn Mountains.
Find a spot to throw out thoughts. Blow my worries to the southwinds.
As clouds are creeping, so is time. There's plenty of daylight left to spare.
I turn up LeDoux a notch or two. His 'Western Skies' drift through the air.
Feeling the freedom of a soaring eagle, while I'm grounded to the road.
A two-track trail away from Hell to replenish my neglected soul.
Some ponderosas are waving me down, so I pull the Chevy over.
I kill the engine as I think out loud, "I could stay up here forever."
Heaven-on-Earth is where I'll be, in case you need to find me.
Right on top. Just look up. Perched on the backbone of Wyoming.

Depending On The Whether

I woke up feeling almost blue, like the sky this time of day.
Ain't no telling if it'll rain or shine. But I'm up, and sat up straight.
I make it to my feet with a foggy head. That'll clear-up before noon.
Fried up some eggs with a side of toast. No longer vodka in my orange juice.
Birds barely chirping out my front door. Sunlight is still struggling to rise.
Hard to make a plan when it depends on whether, under western skies.
Whether or not I've got cash for gas. Because I know I'm good on grass.
Whether or not C-10's ready to run. Open it up and haul some ass.
Whether or not the sun shines on me, either way, I'm getting lit.
By the light of a fire. Wind at my back. Another mountain trip.

Winds of Wyoming

Wyoming winds, please carry me there. Whip me through God's April sky.
Would you carry the weight of a wretched soul, and let me hitch a ride?
With blistering speed we may have a chance. Perhaps we could outrun time?
Sweep the meadows. Chute through valleys. Whistle between the pines.
Plant my foot on the weathered wood-steps to that chapel beneath the mountain.
I cannot hold my peace if I know she is looking at him doubting.
Relentless and cold. But you are, too. You and I are one-in-the-same.
From Sundance to Pinedale, Cheyenne to Sheridan; across high rugged plains.
You're stubborn like me, and I've now seen how fast a heart-of-stone can sink.
Into a sea of regret, eclipsed by the depth, for what could be eternity.
You helped create this beautiful land, with a hand from God-given water.
I know you know the fastest route. Come on, please help me stop her!
Strong and true. Isn't that what you do? Act like thunder... let's get rolling.
Please carry me home. I've no wings to unfold. Oh, won't you, Winds of Wyoming?

Blue Eyes To Match My Collar

Grease, dirt, mud and muck, polyurethane, blue-steel rust.
Paint, caulk, hay, weeds, insulation, shit, and drywall dust.
There are so many things that have their way about covering my body.
Working hard to make someone pay. Looking like this is not pure-hobby.
Sweat and pain. Grit and strain. A little filth to earn a dollar.
I was not born with a silver spoon, but with blue eyes to match my collar.

Lead to Roam

Took a trip upon the mountain. Got off the highway via two-track road.
Found a spot to throw it in park. Stashed your stress. Now you're ready to go.
Two steps out and you're in the wild. Rocky Mountains, so you already know,
You've come to wander, you've found the place. Where all roads lead to roam…
Gridless-miles roaming wild for as far as the eye can see.
Can't help but to shine a brilliant smile, like the sun you stand beneath.
Life is good when the only aisles are the ones hidden among the trees.
So remote with just an axe to file. Where Fahrenheit's the only degrees.
Embrace biophilia, that natural feeling. Sense Mother Nature calling your name.
Let her take you by the upper-hand. She'll help guide the way.
Helluva destination. High elevation. And telling signs that clearly read:
'Right to Roam'; 'No Californication'; 'Take Your Trash With You When You Leave'

Last Stone Turned

Between angels and demons, nothing was even.
Except for the chance to console.
For the good of evil, at times all was abandoned.
I slipped into a dark, cold, vacant hole.
I was sitting rock-bottom. Merely a hidden cricket.
Until that angel lifted the stone.
I was down in the dirt. I could barely chirp.
And she showed up to guide me home.
Her bright light shone like a fiery beacon,
Right through my reckless soul.
Scattering the darkness, I had nowhere to run;
Shed to find my lost control.
That was back when self-will wouldn't let me.
The weight of that boulder had a hold.
But nowadays I know she helped turn the tables,
Not just that heavy stone.

Top of the World

Weaving through the woods I ascended the mountain, to the edge of a canyon wall.
A pair of formidable cliffs accented with ledges. Between them snowmelt still falls.
As the bellowing burbles emit from below, they're also echoing down the chamber.
I've come up here to replenish my soul. Pay a visit to Mother Nature.
Her voice kept calling so naturally. It's the only thing I want to hear.
A couple clouds strolled by, but weren't as high, as I am between my ears.
I came fully prepared with three strong arms, in addition to grit and wit.
I am not rich. I don't want to be famous. Yet, on top of the world here I sit.
I planted to ponder, read and write, whilst the sun got carried away.
Across the blue overhead abyss, before prompting stars to gaze.
Aromas of sage and pine combine. The latter has become light.
Smoke climbs into darkness. Disappears. Like I have, into the night.

Deep Roots

Wide open spaces beneath weathered faces. Manifold mountains scattered about.
Everloving land, under evergreens standing evermore devout.
Sunrise to shine with every dawn. Lay with each sun set silhouette.
Blanket of stars thrown to cover the sky, draping the restless West.
Life's fulfilled in The Big Empty. Up here living out montane dreams.
Deluged with delight by any moonlit creek, or shimmering sun-kissed stream.
Worthwhile wildlife drifting with earth, wind, water, and stone.
Providing life with ample fortune, and fire within my soul.
Where rock formations are destinations and nameless lakes are known.
Where canyons crawl and meadows sprawl to yet another aspen grove.
I was born to die in the Three-O-Seven. I pray to fall where my roots do keep.
After all this is my Heaven, and those fuckers are buried deep.

Headquartered in Headwaters

We've risen to the pinnacle in good company,
My determined brother and I.
We're delegating desires and reaching projections.
Seeing results in reel-time.
Netting enough to keep food on the table.
While keeping an eye on the line.
Opportunities offered are often and equal.
Hell, even the flies are tied.
Maintaining attitudes to match the altitude,
In natural surroundings and open skies.
We met up at headquarters, in headwaters,
And we've been fishing down the mountain side.

Midnight Prairie

Down a road. No place to go. Right back where she left off.
Taking her mind on an evening stroll. A little more wandering than lost.
She basked in yet another sunset, choosing to linger till the stars appear.
Again, she marveled at marbling skies, standing beneath a twilight chandelier.
But as the pale moonlight shone to glow, she carried on her way,
Across a Western sky in which she climbed; free from all restraints.
Floating on the effervescence of a life a lot less weighted.
She waited a lifetime to spread her wings. She's now every bit as weightless.
Her enchanted soul saddled up the wind amid a dim midnight prairie,
Scorching the sky with a blaze in her eyes, wielding reins of lucidity.

Rock Bottom

Canyons, creeks, and mountain peaks, all in correlation with the rain.
Sleet, hail, snow, and the wind that blows, too, have a hand in play.
The bits at the bottom were once at the top, before being swept away.
Under the rug of nature's current. Landing where they'll lay.
Deep in the belly of a canyon forever, most likely to be settled in place.
Never to rise once more, yet this rock-bottom is one magnificent place to stay.

Rising Son

In the early hours of a new day the morning moon begins to fade.
Rolling over peaks, beyond the horizon. Daylight chasing it away.
The house is quiet inside and out, but I've a feeling it's almost time.
I hear him stirring under his sheets... My son's about to rise.
My rising son, from a twin-size bed, where he'll lay down again tonight,
Lights up my life twenty-four-seven, and, man, his light is bright.
He doesn't yet know it, but one day he'll see, I've been shedding mine upon him.
I hope I have shone the best of me. Not too much shade, and I'll be honest,
My rising son, that brilliant boy, he's light years ahead of me.
A brighter star; a warmer heart; an amazing human being.
Capable of climbing any mountain, and confidently deflects doubting.
So curious to take wild peaks. His understanding is astounding.
My rising son has raised my spirit, each day he's blessed my life.
Without him, my skies would darken. For he is my sole son-light.

Summer Nights in Style

Moonlight breaking, quietly making the night a little brighter.
Me plus two; the moon and you. Hanging out, pulling over-nighters.
Breathtaking view with my eyes on you, as they're drawn to your smile.
Way out here with only God to fear, across every country mile.
What we do, well, that's up to you, but let's make it worth your while.
This time of year the sky is crystal clear. We're living summer nights in style.

Heart Within

In his arms, he's picked them up. In their minds, he's let them down;
Countless times, each and the other. Someday he'll make them proud.
One handsome son, two beautiful daughters; three awfully intelligent kids.
One life to live, three more to shape; forever from his heart within.
Instilling self-worth, courage, and kindness. And faith in all the above.
Admitting to his children if he's been wrong; despite possessing tough-love.
From tying their shoes and fixing boo boos, to one day walking young women down the aisle.
Two beautiful brides. One dad set aside; scolding each groom like a child.
And as for his boy, by then a man. And like his sisters, planting new roots.
He'll be shaking his hand, instead of the sand from his well-trodden little boots.
Though a dad's obligations do not end there. His last hope for them is to outlive him.
With silverlined souls and pride laced spirits. Happy. Healthy. Committed.

Lightning Strike

Dove head first. Became submersed. Started drowning in her eyes.
The only thing to pull me out was the savior in her smile.
My heart then floated in her presence. My soul, never as grounded.
A nameless beauty stood before me. To ever speak her name, I doubted.
Much like a river when it meets the sea, she all but up and vanished.
Her scent remained, as I lingered in pain. All hope for her was banished.
Never spoke a word, though I can hear her voice rattle around the chambers,
Of my mind. She was trapped inside, just as life outside reclaimed her.
Was she an angel? Or a ghost? Perhaps just more tantalizing than most?
She was here then gone; a lightning strike.
And, I? Merely a post.

Backroad Retreat

You work all week just to earn a buck. Turn around and pass it on.
Bottles ain't cheap, the truck is thirsty, too. You get paid, and then it's gone.
Throwing punches at the clock by the end of the day. Knockout right at five.
Sure the sun will go down in a little bit, but the weekend is on the rise.
It's Friday night and we don't give a damn. Just let the whiskey flow.
Backroad retreat. Boots and bare feet, once the girls are ready to go.
We'll give it hell and light it up, till church on Sunday morning.
Filling up cups. Twisting some up. Smoke rolling. Spirits pouring.
Beneath the stars is where we are. No city lights to block the view.
Out here with the nighttime breeze, and speakers speaking Chris LeDoux.
Wide open spaces. We're free to roam, as wild as wild can be.
Where everyone around is country grown, and leads a life so free.
It's times like this you try to memorize, oh, only if you could.
All tuned up with good friends around, so the pictures should turn out good.
Partying like it's 1999 to pass the fuck out in the end.
Wake up somewhere tomorrow morning and do it all again.

Blue-Collar Bill

My son was hurting for some cash,
He said "Dad what can I do?
Please give me something, anything,
I can get it done for you.
I will pull the weeds and clean up the trash,
All around the lot.
Stack some wood, or gather rocks.
All I need is just one shot."
My smile stretched a country mile.
I was so damn proud of my young boy.
But I had to wonder what it would be,
Delivering this five-year-old some joy.
He worked all day. He earned his pay.
Oh, the way it made me feel.
To watch my son apply and work,
For his first blue-collar bill.
He lit up over that ten bucks.
It was worth the thirty minutes.
We went to the store, he bought a little toy,
And a six-pack of mini doughnuts.
The look on his face, as we left that place,
Was nothing short of pride.
On our way home, I heard him whisper,
"I suppose work's alright."
Later that night, while we were eating dinner,
As I told his mom about our day,
He piped up, exclaimed, "I love my toy,
But I think next time I'll save.
If I collect a couple hundred-dollars,
I could buy a house that's just for me.
So, is there anything else I can do for you?"
We just laughed, and said "We'll see".

Mother Nature's Daughter

Her long hair flows like a nameless river,
Swaying to meet her feet.
A tantalizing torrent of natural beauty.
Her allure turns men weak.
When her scent of heaven floods the limbic system,
And endorphins come rushing in,
You'll have no chance. She'll steal your breath.
Like a bitter winter wind.
But when you fall, true as the days of Autumn,
There's a chance she'll catch you off guard.
She could break open. Mirror majestic meadows.
And warm up to your charm.
If things heat up, she can take you higher.
Moral heights you'd never before.
While you rapidly rise, both free and wild.
High as an eagle, you'll soar.
Yet, she carries the power to put you down.
Just a wilted-heart back on the ground.
And your mind may make it to what it thinks is shelter,
But Mother Nature's daughter is always around.

Cowboy Carousel

'Round and 'round, up and down. A wild lifestyle he's been living.
8 seconds at a time. Hand-wrapped leather and rawhide rigging.
In the dirt, he does his work, with his hat pulled down real tight.
To win it all he cannot fall. He needs to please a crowd each night.
He pays his fees. To ride ain't free, so he's been sleeping in cheap hotels.
Always on the road with his bag in tow. Riding the Cowboy Carousel.
He won't be eating fancy dinners, unless he buckles down.
Golden lining surrounds it all, as the ride keeps spinning around,
His Nocona boots are missing loops. His chaps are rubbing thin.
His only goal deep in his soul is to hold on for the win.
On the back of a bucking horse. A gripping battle, pound-for-pound.
His sole hope is to find pay-dirt, once the final Finals buzzer sounds.
To make his name in this game he has to fight to stay on top.
Keep his sights on the Hall of Fame. To become immortalized when his ride stops.

Western Star

Once upon a moonlit mountain, I pray to the stars my soul to keep.
Placed perhaps near The Seven Sisters, somewhere out above that cryptic steep;
Who've rose to blossom in this dawn of winter, bearing brilliance in their shine.
Although any sky that overlooks Wyoming, to me, would be divine.
That's where the wind tends to fan my fire; breathing life to my sanguine soul.
So cast me beyond snow capped peaks. Make these Western skies my home.
For if I may become a star, privileged enough to pierce the sky.
Parish to rise into Wyoming nights. I'm a Wyomingite dying to die.

Hands of Time

Some say that age is just a number, but you can see the wrinkle lines.
Truth be told, they tell a story. Upon restless hands of time.
Weathered hands that have paid their dues. Scraped up, broke, or bruised.
Swinging hammers and turning wrenches. Piling hay bales to the moon.
In time the lines remind the hands, every crease was earned.
Much like the calluses and some scars, courtesy of branding iron burns.
Non-stop, around the clock. Working hands that have been dealt.
Through all the pain day-after-day. And all the other things they've felt.
Two hands that've driven countless miles, all across this Western land.
Signed the line on bank loans and bills. Annual taxes to pay the man.
The wrinkles on those worn out hands come from a lifetime of doing work.
Plus changing diapers, cooking dinners, doing dishes, and sweeping dirt.
Tough, yet tender, without a doubt. Surely some good sized gloves to fill.
Yes, my mother's hands are beautiful. Always have been, and always will.

Daddy's Boy

Ever since I can remember, people often like to say,
"You sure are your daddy's boy, you talk and act the same."
Well I've always taken it as a compliment, even standing here today.
Because if who I am, is like my old man, I guess I'll be okay.
He worked all day to earn his pay, outdoors in all the weather.
Rain, sleet, hail, or snow. The summer heat wasn't any better.
Building fences or laying highways. Playing with blue-collared toys.
I owe what I know a lot to him. A young disciple is his boy.
A wife and kids to support and feed, so a difference between want and need.
He had told me without a word, you've gotta work 'cause nothing's free.
I can hear his voice when I speak, and utter any words he says.
Thirty years we are apart. At times it doesn't seem as spread.
I know he wants the best for me, that's why he's done the things he's done.
I will pass that on down the line, and do the same for his grandson.

Square State of Mind

I've been gone for too damn long. I'm sure the wild was worried all week.
I've been longing for fresh mountain-air. Forever West in Wyoming.
The Square State is the only place my shackled mind can be set free.
Truth be told, it's the only place I believe this cowboy ever needs.
Square State of mind. Let the daze unwind, within a pine aroma breeze.
Western Meadowlarks sing their song, whilst whistling wind whips through the trees.
Nature tunes in sync with the view, while I meander like a cut-banked creek.
Coyotes and crickets keeping company, under sparkling stars of the mid-night scene.
It's been a ride, but I'm done with inside, of people, and blacktopped streets.
I don't need a reason, but there are fish that need feeding. Square State of mind retreat.

Innocent Sparkles

Innocent sparkles fill her eyes.
Rosy cheeks surround her smile.
Laughter from the tip of her tongue.
I'll gladly listen for a while.
Long, dark brown, swirly curls,
Rest upon her busy head.
Growing fast, like a weed.
Learning from everything that's said.
She's 3 feet tall, and 35 pounds,
But she's a giant where she stands.
'Cause she's the biggest part of my life,
As hers is in my hands.
Not yet the dad I want to be,
But I'm doing good, I think.
If all else fails, to make her happy,
I'll buy her something pink.
Since the day I met her mother,
I knew I'd be her father.
She's so smart and full of wonder.
Forever my beautiful daughter.

Prairie Princess

Pride of the prairie. Predestined to ride. She was born with a silver saddle.
Filled to the brim of her hat with beauty, a pinch of love, and a ton of mettle.
Her father is king of twelve-thousand acres. Her mother; the caboodle's Queen.
A whole-damn-lot of some of the prettiest country a cowboy has ever seen.
She spends most days meandering meadows, in the buckskin valley of her swayback horse.
She keeps out the world by latching the gates, using wire loops of high-tensile force.
The sun and the stars suit her best, so no need for a big old castle.
So dear to her heart are the ways of the West. From cleaning stables to branding cattle.
And only fools would assume that little cowgirls clearly cannot clear leather.
A .38 on her hip, and carrying true-grit. She'd rule this world if only God let her.
She can drown the sound of a raging river. She's the reason flowers bloom.
She's the one to whom the birds are singing, and why coyotes cry at the mid-night moon.
She weathers the storm in any weather, whether up the mountain or amid her plains.
After all, she's the Prairie Princess, so the forecast calls for reign.

First Time Out the Gate

In the chute, and a cowboy hat, with light-up sneakers on my feet.
I wrapped my arms. Secured a grip. Cried "I can ride this smelly sheep!"
It was County Fair, but the battle wasn't. The mutton busted and laid me straight.
My dad then said, "Son, don't you worry, 'cause that's your first time out the gate."
That first time was surely special. I didn't know what to expect.
I just went with the flow, and by the end I'd know, next time's a better bet.
Inflated pride, given by a try. Embracing the old cowboy way.
I just brushed it off with a shit-eating grin. Survived to ride another day.
At four-foot tall and bulletproof, a lesson learned that has stuck with me.
You start by starting. Simple as that. Gotta earn the hat to ride the sheep.

Mountain Meadow Green

It ain't in Paris. Or the Hawaiian islands. It's this place that I call home.
Laying on my chest, staring back at me. That's why you're the background on my pho
And it's no surprise your rolling eyes have kept this engine moving.
I don't mind that they have me hypnotized. I'll do whatever they want me doing.
It may sound cliche, but anyway, you've the prettiest eyes I've ever seen.
Skyline blue looks good on you, 'cause they're mountain meadow green.
I know those wildflowers in your hair set everything up just right,
But the most beautiful sight that a man can seek is still found inside those eyes.
Every ounce of my being belongs to you, at least that's how mine see it.
Every ounce of your being is flawless and true. Even perfectionists believe it.
Every evening, they drive me home. Each morning, late to work.
They've watched me at my best of times. They've seen me at my worst.
I don't know why, but I'm glad they do, somehow see something in me.
I'm forever grateful for all that you do, and your mountain meadow greens.

All Shapes & Sizes

Beyond the years between his ears, my Little Man wears no cape.
Yet hanging on a hero's hook, in his room, I've seen it draped.
In his eyes I may be the man; a boy, if he only knew.
He is the one, my only son, I have always looked up to.
Heroes come in all shapes and sizes, at times they even cry.
Like when their favorite book gets torn, or you forget to sing a lullaby.
They will surprise you, and also remind you of the reasons why,
You can be a mighty superhero even though you cannot fly.
Saving lives countless times, each day, for play and real.
I thought I was to be the hero, though the opposite, I feel.
No, all heroes do not wear capes. Some look like little boys;
Playing cars upon his knees, surrounded by his toys.
Or scaling eye-height countertops, as his mama's heart gets attacked.
But he laughs at danger. He shows no fear, when a pillowcase has got his back.
He likes to dress-up like a peg-legged pirate, or anyone else his mind pretends,
And it may just be a cowboy costume, but my hero, he has always been.

For Heaven's Sake

For Heaven's sake I hope they know they have an angel on the loose.
From what I've seen, I do believe she's one they can't afford to lose.
Her halo is hidden beneath the hood of my old sweatshirt as it rains.
Her hand has landed in the palm of mine, so I'll hold on for Heaven's sake.
For Heaven's sake, my sole hope is that God cannot feel pain.
For if He can, He feels it now. Frantic in front of Faith and Grace.
A faulted wing with a faultless heart. God-given stars in her angel eyes.
And they happen to see something in me that appears to mirror her shine.
As the rain keeps falling, as do I. His tears land upon our shoulders.
She ain't homesick, as I presume He is. She's done what her heart had told her.
In the wake of Heaven's mistake; by the grace of God, one slipped away,
I'm giving thanks, while sending my thoughts; praying for Heaven's sake.

The Other Side

Stashed with spirits near a hole-in-the-wall. Hidden in the bowels of a slithering canyon.
Lightning illuminates rain glazed faces. Such a riveting intoxication.
Thunder rolls through the steeped ravine, like a musket ball through a barrel.
Booming under phantom skies, to attest the canyon's mettle.
On a bend beneath a jutting bluff. The western flank without a trail.
The eastern slope is my only hope, to climb out of this living hell.
Been down deep for two damn days and then the Fork began to climb.
There's no fucking way this is how I go; dying to get to the other side.
Roaring currents rapidly rise into a black veil of ominous sky.
My grip is slipping. No breath to catch. I let go and close my eyes.

Small Town Sunset

You've captured my eye like a midnight moon. The setting sun and I are falling.
Below His hand-painted neon sky, street lights flicker, and the night starts calling.
Crickets and the breeze to serenade you, amidst the bloom of a western June.
I hold reservations about being indoors, yet I'd sit with you in any room.
Hell, you could hold me up and take my time. If you'd spend it all in town and country.
Where Memory Lane is every street, and strewn throughout are parts that made me.
Local Ma & Pa's are currently closed but the open range is 24/7.
We can head out there, take 'em all in; breathtaking prospects of heaven.
As the sun parts-way with another day your troubles can leave town with it.
Ain't nothing out here to fret or fear, but keep an eye on the small-town sunset.
Then you and I beneath a starry blanket, all covered up in the Western sky.
In the morning, if you're not long-gone, we'll feast our eyes on a stellar sunrise.

Wyoming Widow

Peak-shaped shadows cast over a valley peppered with black angus and sage.
The sun is crawling behind the silhouette. Intermission to the cowgirl's day.
She hasn't been sleeping, because it's calving season. And neither have her kids.
Their father perished in an accident. Holding up the ranch has come down to them.
A Wyoming widow, without her right-hand man, in heated battles against the snow.
The frigid wind, and dead-of-night, keep her stifled from a bed so cold.
She'll protect her land till Hell freezes over, with a loaded rifle and true grit.
Her kids by her side, helping defend off coyotes, and bankers with their bullshit.
She is one tough mother, working so damn hard, devoting her life to others.
Selflessly determined to never have to wonder, if they'll ever lose the land he's under.

Old Porch Swing

The old weathered chains that keep it up have been holding on for years.
Supporting all the heavy weight of three generation's hopes and fears.
The cracks throughout its splintered wood catch family secrets and some tears.
Countless stories and sunrise mornings since my dad's dad hung it here.
The nuts and bolts are rusted threads, and some are even missing.
But what it means to all of us are memories and reminiscing.
It was built way back in '53 when he was short on cash for a diamond ring.
So he just asked, "Will you grow old with me?"
While they were sitting on her new porch swing.
Though, not just a bench to sit and talk,
But to lend an ear to listen, too.
Over broken hearts, and celebration.
As well as the coyotes cry to the Autumn moon.
The armrests have held all kinds of hands.
Mostly kinship to have come through.
Just stopping by, maybe staying the night,
It's a tradition Grandma liked to do.
Now I brought you here to the homestead swing,
Not solely to rest your feet.
Or to tell you a story of my grandparents,
Even though it's so damn sweet.
I brought you here to extend a proposal,
So I'm truly elated you think it's neat.
Before this swing, between you and me,
I've a question I'd like to repeat.
"Decades have passed since '53,
Yet in '55 he gave his queen her ring.
Here it is... will you grow old with me?,
I ask for your hand, like Grandma's old porch swing."

One Night Downtown

Met a young woman one night downtown,
We commenced conversing over Crown.
I spilt a little, she got upset. I had to chase her cute ass down.
Looking back now, we have a good laugh,
The both of us, still hanging around.
But she had a daughter, so when I caught her,
Two, was what I found.
A couple of pieces that became parts of me,
And in time our family will grow.
She'll become a big sister,
To a baby brother... she claims to hope.
But for now I'm goin' to learn the ways,
Of what makes 2-year-old girls happy.
Like flying kites, riding bikes,
Losing the belongings to every Barbie.
It doesn't matter what she calls me,
She just needs to know I love her.
And I hope I do good by her,
By the way I treat her mother.
I'm checking for monsters each and every night,
Burning Eggos every morning.
And there is no mistaken, it is my heart,
Not just my hair she's been adorning.

Barebacks and Bank Bags

Robbing banks along the banks of the wide and wild Missouri.
Across Montana, down the Dakotas, busting ass back West to ol' Wyoming.
Hell bent for leather with three-hundred horses galloping down barren backroads.
On the run, and there ain't no stopping, unless this screaming engine blows.
Staying off the highways as much as possible. The CB's loud and clear.
I have no idea what time it is, but sundown's already here.
Headed for our own hole-in-the-wall, I know a place by Powder River.
It's about time to ditch these guys. It's too goddamn late to reconsider.
Bail on-out if you can't keep on, but good luck keeping your money.
And them ain't law-dogs chasing our tail, these badgering bastards are after honey.
I have a place in mind that we can break loose. The road splits in a few directions.
I'll kill the lights and pull a hard right, throwing a loop back behind them.
Bolt to the barn of the first ranch we see, and rustle a couple of barebacks.
Won't have saddles but hell-bent we'll be, with these two duffels full of bank bags.

Between You and Me

I'm jealous of this mountain breeze as it floats across your smile.
But I'm still hoping that maybe we could just stay up here a while.
Let's get closer. I want to know you. Tell me all your hopes and dreams.
Where'd you come from? How's your Mama? What makes you still believe?
Does your daddy know where you are? Sitting beside me in this truck?
Right here on the edge of this pond, his daughter with a lucky duck.
Nights like this are the best goodnights, 'cause sweet dreams are coming true.
I have your name. I don't need your number, but only 'cause I'm already with you.
How's a girl like you end-up out here, wrapped inside my country arms?
Must have caught you when you fell, from the angel forge among the stars.
Between you and me, that space between us has gotten awfully slim.
The two of us are casting one shadow. Not even moonlight can slide in.

While I'm Alive

A long-lived life is a life I long for. I guess you'll find out in the end.
Everyday I rise for false hope from my bed. What if time was a friend instead?
For when the day comes, and Death shows for my soul, just know that I didn't oblige.
My flesh and bones were merely on loan but for the soul I paid full price.
Caring deeply for my family and friends. Enjoying music, a few sports, and marijuana.
I always worked real hard to feel fulfilled. NOT to pay cyclical bills I didn't wanna.
I loved the outdoors and the state in which I was born; the only places worth calling home.
I never liked crowds, congested cities, social media, or addiction to phones.
My wishes are simple: turn me to ash, then let me fly in the Wyoming wind.
From up on the pass of the Bighorn Mountains. A Powder River precipice.
At the end of it all, I hope you're proud of the man, if one were to speak my name.

Then again, even while alive, I do hope it's much the same.

Winds of Change

The day we met, I met my match.
It didn't take much to light the flame.
Romance tore through like a raging fire,
Without a prayer to send the rain.
We danced all night, as flames tend to do.
Only the past remained contained.
Consumed by desire. She took me higher,
But the winds-of-change are who's to blame.

A Gentle Touch

At twenty-five you're so alive, but you don't know what quite for.
The good times call. You rise and fall. Then she walks through the door.
In that moment your heart speaks up, tells you she's the one.
After that, the rest is history, yet far from being done.
She stole your heart, your body, and soul. Your name was the last thing she took.
She cleaned you out without a doubt, but you let her off the hook.
Because in exchange she's given you your children and your home.
A gentle touch doesn't seem like much, but from it a family's grown.
As time goes by you learn what not to do, but still wonder who you are.
A beautiful mess nonetheless, yet everyday you raise your bar.
Four bedroom house up on the hill, with the mortgage paid on time.
A front porch swing to rest her feet. The hill was worth the climb.
A life together. Is there anything better? Even when times start to get tough.
Quickly stop the clock. Listen, then talk. And make sure you've done enough.
Don't ever give up on love and faith. Do be faithful to your love.
Sent from above to be the one and only fingerprint of that touch.

Lucky Man

I love the way her favorite shoes walked right into my life.
Two years later, a pair to match the dress as she became my wife.
It's been a while since the wedding aisle, but she's more beautiful each day.
When people tell me I'm a lucky man, all I can do is grin and say...
"Out of billions of people in the world, I may have struck a little luck.
Her eyes are more like sparkling diamonds. and she has a golden touch.
Her body itself is a gem. Always shining under the sun.
To everyone else she may be a ten, but to me she is the one.
She stole my heart fair and square, although I gave her my surname.
To me she's worth everything; more than money; more than fame.
Someone to love, laugh with, and carry, through all life's ups and downs.
Seems to me, it's easy to see, I'm the luckiest man around.
Since she's been wrapped up in my life, I hit the jackpot every night.
Laying in bed, waking up again, with my winnings to my right."

Love Junkie

Both inside and out, she's beautiful. 100% pure love.
Seeing her smile drives me wild. No one gets to me like she does.
She's my every goodmorning and each goodnight. Everything in between.
Even when I sleep, laying by her side, she's the woman of my dreams.
I can't get enough of her love. I am addicted to her touch.
Always wanting more. She's what I look for. Unable to possess too much.
Forever is a long ass time, but it could never be long enough,
To drain the desire I have for her, or to make me give her up.
Clearly irreversible. There's no help for me. I hear acceptance is the key.
I guess this is who I am. An old love junkie. And proud to be.

A Milestones Throw

Sitting on the tailgate gazing at the stars, then my darling dropped the news.
She was pregnant, and she had been since the latter part of June.
To my surprise, my first thought was about playing peek-a-boo.
With my son, or my daughter. No matter at all, pink or blue.
There were changes coming. I wasn't running. I was right there by her side.
So much pride had built up inside, this family man broke down and cried.
A little addition to our life, meant big responsibilities.
But to become a dad was my wish come true. Living out my wildest dream.
A few months later she went into labor, and gave birth to a handsome son.
With what God gave her, she did me a favor. I've always known she was the one.
My entire heart was in that bed, although clearly no longer mine.
The purest moment in my fortunate life, as she hummed sweet lullabies.
By 3 a.m. I never rested my head. He was having a pretty rough night.
I rocked again. We nodded off to sleep as I whispered "Everything's alright."
Fast forward five fast years, now we're at the school for his first day.
A lot of crying. No denying. Other than that, his mom did okay.
Kids running around, I say "Let him go, and make a new best friend."
Another milestone thrown our way. Welcome to Kindergarten.

Right Back

Man in the Moon, I'm counting on you to brighten up my night.
She took off, and it won't be long till her tail lights are out of sight.
You're way up there with a birds-eye view. At times a great spotlight.
And I think I know where she is going. She's about to take a right.
Right back to her Mama's place.
Right there in our hometown.
Right back to before she was mine.
Right before her homecoming crown.
Right back to her old bedroom.
Right up those stairs that she'd sneak down.
Right back to something we once knew.
Right out of my life somehow.
Over the years we had shared our fears, but I failed to mention this,
To have her leave was my greatest one. I'd much rather be penniless.
Moving on will take some time, but I'll need endless time to heal.
There's a gaping hole inside of me that she no longer fills.

Behind Your Binky

"I'm wrapped around your little finger, much like the ring I gave your mom.
Two months old. You have the purest soul, and have made my heart your home.
You are not my first, or my only, but you will surely be my last.
Then again, I'm all three to you; one lucky man you know as Dad.
As you grow older you will see how much your Mama truly means.
To me and you, your siblings too. She's every root of the family tree.
So sturdy and strong. She is one proud Mom. Daddy feels the same.
It's more than love, more than trust. More to a family than just a name.
Surround yourself with beautiful people, and I mean beneath the surface.
Search for joy in everything you do, because life is far from perfect.
Build resilience to fight your fights. Don't be afraid to fall.
Stand up tall with confidence. Take proper steps to skip the crawl.
Baby Girl, there may come a day when you won't need me by your side.
If I ever say that I'm fine with that, please just know that Daddy lied.
I'm gonna teach you so many things about Western land and life.
I'm excited to watch you find your way, in-time as you learn to fly.
Yes, a lot of thoughts cloud my head... So what have you been thinking?"
I ask blue-eyes staring back at me, as you just smile behind your binky.

Made In Wyoming

Bedded down beneath the mountains, lies the origin of my being.
As my first-steps were amid the foothills in Johnson County, Wyoming.
Like the Bighorn Mountains, I was born and raised under western skies.
And I'll live my whole life in this country. Powder River is where I'll die.
From cowboys and cowgirls of this great state, to the iron oxide in Yellowstone,
God may bless the Cowboy State, but it's with what Natives have always known.
The healing powers of the great outdoors. Elevate life with the rising sun.
It's an honor to be made in Wyoming. The heart of what I've come to love.

Mountain Time

Wild turkey from a roost, gobbling to the dew.
Floating down from a branch; a switch to ground-level view.
The day is up and on its way to establishing rhythm and rhyme.
It couldn't care less what a clock has to say, not here in Mountain Time.
Where hands get dealt, right after breakfast, their chore lists for the day.
It's tiresome work; working off the lineup. Sweat equity is duly gained.
Living with purpose, pleasure or passion, so long as its treated with pain,
Is a life worth spending all your time refusing to wither away.
There's a spotlight shone on Mountain Time all throughout the year;
Finding all four seasons to lose oneself makes the rest disappear.
A clear sky much like my conscience; through the trees the sky is blue.
A creek creeps through a shady canyon, waiting for another storm to roll through.
I simply can't say enough about the mountain, and the highs it has brought to me.
Mountain Time is a state of mind within the state of mine, Wyoming.

Eclipsed

Suspended from a moonless sky until your mom brought you to life.
I understand now, you're not just my son; you're a collection of my light.
How little girls dream of their wedding day, I admittedly dreamt of you.
Although I adore and would kill for your beautiful sisters, too.
You're my only boy to help carry our name; help make Grandpa and Uncle proud.
To show without saying, I'll do my best to never let you down.
Independent, yet empathetic; two traits from me and your mom.
A magnetic smile. The most curious child. And the list goes on and on.
One day we'll stand eye-to-eye; the time will arise for me to reflect.
If I hope to see the best parts of me, I stand to lay what's left to rest.
Tighten my tongue and straighten my path. I vow to keep our mountain moving.
You and the girls are Dad's moon, stars and world, plus the skies Mom hung you in.

Heart Broke

A mild stallion and a wildflower, together on the open plains.
Storm rolled in, engulfed their light. Each ill-prepared to become tamed.
Only time would tell if the love could last inundated with indignation.
Coming to grips, they let devotion slip, faster than lightning sparks ignition
Understanding went out to pasture, and faith was soon to follow.
Pride took a dive into the mire, and lathered-up to wallow.
No knowledge from experience. No patience for time to train.
Just a stupefied jackass standing there; heart-broke in the rain.

Tin-Can Alley

Cascading down to meet the river; a lofty bank of sandstone bluffs.
Badland beauty beyond the cusp. Hares tucked beneath sagebrush.
Home to snakes and lizards, cacti and critters. Housing a nostalgia for childhood.
I'd take memory lane to old Tin-Can Alley, oh, if only today's wheels could.
Loaded up on bikes, we'd shoot for the cattle guard, pedal to the top of the bridge.
Fireworks and firearms in our presence, such a gift to a latchkey kid.
Days of freedom for a few young men out exploring the great outdoors.
We were on the run - once they were done - from the torture of indoor chores.

Horsing Around

Five days spent up on the mountain. Thirteen-plus years in the making.
Saddled-up beside my Grandpa, after over thirteen years of waiting.
Sitting taller than I have ever sat. Teenage spirit skyward bound.
Only thing better than being in the mountain... is being in the mountain while horsing around.
An experience that's at-one with the landscapes. The pair, so wildly serene.
Where morale mirrored the mountain meadows, I reflect upon a lived out dream.
Light on the heart. Heavy on bliss. A high concentration of grace.
Rain clouds in the distance. Reins in my hand. Shit-eating grin upon my face.

Forgiveness

Things don't sit right once you've been wronged; left standing outside within.
Resentment builds. Happiness crumbles. Somehow forgiveness spoils to sin.
A challenge to most, simply because it's hard to let go, or give for free.
Yet, forgiveness is meant to be spent on oneself. Saving shitloads of misery.
No, it is not meant for the opposing side; contrary to that disbelief.
It starts in your mind and flows to your heart. A personal and prosperous release.
'Cause the one forgiven couldn't care less, either way they're about their day.
You're the one paying the toll, so why would they care if it gets paid?
Always be selfish when it comes to forgiveness, and forgive yourself when given the chanc
For that debt accrued inside of you could have been paid for in advance.

Friends In Low Places

Tucked in tight beside a creek bed. Set-up camp on the canyon floor.
Ushered in by waving waters that live and die by mountain storms.
Hands of time beneath our feet. Blue skies overhead.
Getting high with friends in low places, fishing around another bend.
A few days away to clear the haze, and drown the embers in my mind.
Swapping stories, flinging flies, wading knee-deep with these guys.
I am inundated with allurements. Captivated by nature's call.
Finding ways to decompress between two canyon walls.

Fall From A Peak

Folded layers of bounteous land, golden grass, and evergreens.
A bighorn sheep lounged in the clouds. Snapshot from a September peak.
Stands of quaking aspen have begun to blush, reintroducing the palette of Autumn.
Raspberry red and russet orange. Yellow picked from an arrowleaf's blossom.
If the sky's the limit, I am already there; brushing shoulders with the mountain.
Peeking at the heavens with a naked eye, upon this peak that I have mounted.
I see wide-open meadows and narrow draws, icy slopes and fiery canyons.
As Summer winds down, amid the rising Fall, Winter prowls on the horizon.
Another glance before my descension. What a sensational scene to see.
I may come down and return to town, but I'm rebounding again next Spring.

Body of Work

In the end, the body is a representation of its life's work.
What it has been through. Where has it been? How much so much of it hurt.
Prices paid for the marks obtained, without telling signs of priceless-worth.
Wrinkles; deformities; amputations; birthmarks; scars and burns.
Bookmarks within one's passage, throughout their allotted time,
With each turn of the page another is gained, so again, one's redefined.
At the very least, while it is able, my working-body is a body of work.
It's what I do. I just need to. Until y'all leave me in the dirt.

Neighbor In Need

When a neighbor's in need, hands get dealt.
Helping out in any season.
Grabbing gloves, and starting the truck,
Without having even known the reason.
Out on the road, or in the pasture,
Asking questions for the answer after.
While drinking bourbon, or a beer...
Assuming no need for a pastor.
Any hand lent amends the alliance,
On the occasion for the sake of heart.
Pledge allegiance to cattle country.
God bless cowpokes and the way they are.

Thick As Thieves

Sitting tight in a landlocked basin, skirted by farmland all around.
Fifteen-hundred blue-collared people work everyday-boots into the ground.
Pick a peak in any direction. Mountain views are so profound.
Much like the river flowing through it, the little town is nestled down.
The type of place most pass right by, but to the locals, another round.
Me and some fellas are still thick as thieves. The Boys from my hometown.
From when bikes were good to get us going. They could then keep us there all day.
Finally got a license and started driving. That really paved the way.
With horsepower running down the road, gone is where we'd stay.
Going nowhere was good enough. Headed somewhere changed the game.
In a crew cab Chevy with spare tires and time, always ready to play.
A time or two we were in a pickle, yet still wound up stealing base.
The whole damn gang still gets together, once we devise a master plan.
Hunting, camping, or catch us fishing. Somewhere out holding up the land.
To have grown up with that wild bunch is a true blessing on its own.
Our roots run deep like a ponderosa, and they've been petrified to stone.
We had girls, and we had guns, but we rarely mixed them up.
One was for pleasure. The other for fun. Both utilizing the back of a truck.
Free to roam. We were nineties kids. No social media in our sights.
Where we were at, only God and us knew. Oh, the hell we raised each night.
We have stories that you wish you lived. Others you couldn't believe.
Some you wouldn't wish on your enemy. Great times that forged us thick as
thieves.

Butterfly

The day they met, she was two years old. Her mother witnessed it unfold.
Unbeknownst to the three of them, there was a story to be told.
A shy little girl, merely a toddler, topped off with short brown curls.
Looked up to the man standing before her; who was rearranging his whole world.
Making room for them to stay in his heart for as long as they could.
Clearing space to make a safe place, anywhere they stood.
Standing there on the edge of tomorrow, he took one more good-look around.
Glanced at his future, and in that moment, he found a daughter to make proud.
Two years later, as the story goes, she'd been calling that man her dad.
He couldn't recall a life before he took each young-lady by the hand.
He'd given each one a shiny ring on the day that he proposed.
Hers, a butterfly; emerald green. The mother; a diamond, I suppose.
In his arms she'd set up shelter, with a blanket and a book.
When they weren't too busy dressing-up, perfecting the princess look.
They'd chase down dreams on imaginary horses. Ride just like the wind.
That man hasn't forgotten those precious days.
Oh, where would he even begin?

A Game of Why?

Into a veil of night, time leapt and vanished.
All the while the world beside me.
She was the one; the farmer's daughter;
A bona fide beauty from Wyoming.
Her earth-tone eyes put stars to shame,
Gleaming in caramel light.
A curious damsel, with countless questions,
Although each was merely "Why?"
I had the answers, or thought I did,
So I rattled them off with charm.
I'd stay there forever, if I had to,
Where time doesn't exist in the heart.
Sitting on that porch in the dead of night;
I've yet to again feel that alive.
Nevertheless, the years steadily passed,
Leaving me clueless as to "Why?"

Small Town Sunrise

Alarm clock glowing; the first glimpse of dawn. Feet hit the floor, head out the door.
Roads begin crawling with familiar faces. With each inch climbed the sun ushers mor
Each on their way to work or play, whilst the sky mixes orange and blue.
No red lights to hold us up, just Fords and Chevys rolling through.
A little place you've never heard of, yet more than a one-horse town.
Where regulars at the local Co-op pass stories and coffee around.
All the while school bus No. 9 has been kicking rocks out in the country,
To pick up six kids off-the-grid, that wake up around 4:30.
Folks on Main Street flip their Welcome signs; 'Come On In, We're Open'.
Might have someone soon, or at least by noon is all the owner's hoping.
A brand new day, it's safe to say. Birds commence their leaps to fly.
We slowly make our way inch-by-inch, much like this quiet small-town's sunrise.

Proceed Without Caution

Weak at the knees and barely breathing, when her fingers ran through my hair.
And the way she danced was like no other, even if the whole damn world was there.
If good-looks could kill, sure, she'd be an outlaw but she wouldn't have to run.
She'd shatter hearts like brittle stones, hit on the mark from a smoking gun.
If you asked me what's more plausible, proceeding with caution or roping the wind?
Better fetch me a lasso, because I'd be the asshole ignoring the signs again.
To proceed with caution isn't really an option when you're mid-air from the fall.
I've reached too far. For too long I've listened to her song as the siren calls.
Sounds to be about fatal attraction, and the vast difference between love and lust.
'Cause the love for me she once possessed has lost its luster; shine to rust.
Perhaps it may be polished by passion? Or melted to make a mold?
Through a fury of fire designed by desire. Something far more precious than gold.
I know I shouldn't 'cause another damn hurting is bound to beat me down.
But she might be worth it. Hell, I'm almost certain. I'm down for another round.

Jasper

The golden hues of mookaite jasper, marbled into puppy dog eyes.
Curly coat to match, monstrous paws and claws, but benevolent deep inside.
Impervious passion and loyalty. A good boy beyond belief.
A cuddly crony. A beautiful buddy. And I'm sure he thinks likewise of me.
He is one handsome doodle. More retriever than poodle. Restoring my faith everyday.
On time when I need him. Never a time that I won't. 'Cept when his big ass is in the way.

Meadowlark On A Moose Skull

Peerless peaks of snow-lit granite. Countless colors flood the eyes.
Indian Paintbrush-speckled meadows reflect wildflower skies.
Spellbinding beauty bound in dawn, as summer begins to fall.
Birds are singing while a coyote's cry projects from canyon walls.
Slow rising sun. Fast fading moon. The transition halts at blue.
Air as fresh as the brand new day. Backcountry deer are on the move.
From the treeline an elk appears, sounding off his bugle.
Cued by a Western Meadowlark, perched atop a moose skull.
So much life. So much beauty. Even within the bull's eye socket.
Flora and fauna flourish and rise inside all of Nature's pockets.

Possession

I've never longed for a place in all my life,
Outside of her wide-stretched arms.
A breath of fresh air every time,
While the world's fire rages on.
Born and raised within her beauty;
Beneath her skies; upon her peaks.
I'm just a boy that belongs to Wyoming.
Where there is no vacancy.

Horizons

Entrenched in a canyon, lies the bed of Wind River.
Beneath her mighty headboard, Gannett Peak.
Rise and shine to the highest point, in all the land of Wyoming.
Crisp air dancing on a cool breeze, floating across the sky.
Elevated spirits match the rise. Ghostly clouds coincide.
Nature's glaciers feed lakes and streams, purely as clear can be.
Look over the land like the eye of God, for as far as the eye can see.
A stewardess of great divides; Continental, and the horizons.
Rose to the pinnacle in a land so free, yet in a nation so divided.

Special Thanks and Acknowledgment

Over the course of my 37 years of life, I have been blessed to witness a number of impressive musical artists perform live in Northern Wyoming. I want to give special thanks and shout outs to three of these strangers, yet fellow native sons of 307, for unknowingly bestowing influence upon me. And for representing the Cowboy State in such illustrious fashion. Thank you each for keeping genuine western tradition alive and well...

— Ian Munsick of Sheridan County

— Chancey Williams of Crook County

— And of course, the late and great daddy of 'em all-
Chris LeDoux of Powder River Country

JT Chapman

Milton Keynes UK
Ingram Content Group UK Ltd.
UKHW040836021124
450589UK00001B/63

9 781956 881486